The Joy of Boogie and Blues

THE JOY OF BOOGIE AND BLUES is a collection of thirty-one imaginative piano solos in the early-to-intermediate grades. Some of these pieces are modern settings of standard, ever-popular folk and blues melodies, others are original compositions inspired by and built on certain styles and elements of jazz.

Essentially "blues" and "boogie," as well as "ragtime," "swing," "be-bop," are jazz styles which have emerged on the American musical scene one by one from about the turn of the century to our days. The oldest and most basic of these idioms is the blues. The prototype of the blues is a simple, but characteristic harmonic sequence of twelve measures, divided into three phrases, with a freely improvised, very expressive melody line. It probably is one of the main roots of the entire jazz idiom.

Boogie-Woogie, as developed in the twenties and thirties by Jimmy Yancey, "Pinetop" Smith, Pete Johnson and others, was originally built on the harmonic scheme of the blues. Its mood and tempo, however became quite different: more joyful and more propulsive. The essence of boogie is an ever recurring bass figure, an exuberant "basso ostinato," providing a solid background for a strongly punctuated right hand melody.

It should be noted that boogie, blues and other styles of jazz are not only domains of the popular music field, but also important and typically American contributions to contemporary music in general. The teacher and student of piano will find in this volume a colorful repertoire of most attractive solo pieces which can be integrated with the regular teaching materials with excellent results.

A few suggestions on performance: Use little or no pedal at all, especially in the faster boogie pieces; keep a steady beat throughout, but don't let your playing become stiff; let the music come through with a relaxed, natural lift and "swing."

Distributed throughout the world by Music Sales Corporation
24 East 22nd Street, N.Y. 10010, New York, U.S.A.

78 Newman Street, London W1P 3LA.

27 Clarendon Street, Artarmon, Sydney, N.S.W., Australia.

Printed in Austria

CONTENTS

Blues No. 1

Gerald Martin

Moderately slow

Boogie No. 1

Moderate or lively

Gerald Martin

House of the Rising Sun

Folk Blues
Arr. by Gerald Martin

Old Joe Clark's Boogie

Gerald Martin

Worried Man Blues

Folk Blues
Arr. by Gerald Martin

won't be wor - ried long.

Rolling Stone

Moderately, with a good beat

Gerald Martin

Deep Blue Sea Boogie

Gerald Martin

One - Track Toccata

Gerald Martin

Good Night Boogie

Moderately, with a solid beat

Gerald Martin

Bill Bailey Rag

Hughie Cannon —
Gerald Martin

Hot and Code

Gerald Martin

The Rock Island Line

Arr. by Gerald Martin

Lively "chug-along" tempo

Sailors' Boogie

Gerald Martin

"The Drunken Sailor"

"Blow The Man Down"

The Lonesome Road

Folk Blues
Arr. by Gerald Martin

Timber!

Arr. by Gerald Martin

Lively and robust

Moonshine Sonata

"Real Old Mountain Dew"

Comfortably rolling; with "spirit"

Gerald Martin

grass - es grow and wa - ters flow in a free and ea - sy

way; But give me e-nough of the fine old stuff that's

made near Gal - way Bay. Throw a - way your pills it'll

cure all ills of pa - gan, Christ - ian, Jew, Take

off your coat and free your throat with the real old moun - tain dew.

dew.

ƒ (repeat 𝒑)

ƒ (repeat 𝒑)

dim.

𝑚𝑓 rit.

Blues in C

Comfortable walking tempo

Gerald Martin

Meet Frankie and Johnny

Gerald Martin

Whistling the Blues

Gerald Martin

Spiritual Boogie

Gerald Martin

"Somebody's Knocking At Your Door"

"No Hiding Place" (Variation)

Blue Waltz

Denes Agay

Swingin' Molly

Gerald Martin

Moderately, with a strong beat

The Cotton Mill Blues

Moderately slow

Arr. by Gerald Martin

Jazz Ostinato

Gerald Martin

Safari

Denes Agay

Saint James Infirmary Blues

Gerald Martin

Dark-Eyes Boogie

Gerald Martin

Another Shade of Blue

Denes Agay

Slowly, with a free lilt

Walkin' In The Rain

Gerald Martin

Comfortable walking tempo

Ballad Improvisation

Moderately; free moving

Denes Agay

Honky - Tonky

Gerald Martin